A Voice from the Wilderness

→ THE STORY OF ANNA HOWARD SHAW ←

written & illustrated by
DON BROWN

HOUGHTON MIFFLIN COMPANY
BOSTON 2001

www.houghtonmifflinbooks.com

The text of this book is set in 16-point Bembo.
The illustrations are pen and ink and watercolor on paper.

Library of Congress Cataloging-in-Publication Data
Brown, Don, 1949 –
A voice from the wilderness : the story of Anna Howard Shaw / Don Brown.
p. cm.
ISBN 0-618-08362-6
1. Shaw, Anna Howard, 1847–1919—Juvenile literature. 2. Suffragists—United States—Biography—
Juvenile literature. 3. Woman social reformers—United States—Biography—Juvenile
literature. [1. Shaw, Anna Howard, 1847-1919. 2. Suffragists. 3. Women—Biography.] I. Title.
JK1899.S6 B76 2001   324.6'23'092—DC21   [B]   00-033482

Manufactured in the United States of America
BVG 10 9 8 7 6 5 4 3 2 1

For Sue & David, with love

By most measures, Anna Howard Shaw's life was hard and filled with struggle.

But Anna used her own scale and kept her own measurements, and that made all the difference.

In 1851, four-year-old Anna, her brothers, sisters, and mother left their home in England to join Anna's father. He had emigrated to America nearly two years earlier.

During their voyage aboard the *John Jacob Westervelt,* a terrible storm struck.
The ocean tumbled and tilted, curled and crashed.

The storm raged for three days. When it ended, the broken ship had to be
towed back to England and repaired before it could try the crossing again.

The family's arrival in New York was a joyous shock for Anna's father, who had been told that the *John Jacob Westervelt* had sunk and his family had been lost.

"He could hardly believe that we were really restored to him," Anna wrote many years later. "I can still see the expression in his wet eyes as he picked me up and tossed me in the air."

The Shaws settled in Lawrence, Massachusetts.

There, Anna ate her first banana. She was so unhappy with its taste that she burst into tears. Not knowing better, she had tried eating it unpeeled! It was an unpleasant lesson, but she learned something new.

Lawrence was a place of interesting and educated people. Anna attended school and was happy. Still, Anna's father believed a better life awaited the family in the West. In 1859, Anna's father and her oldest brother, James, traveled to the wilds of Michigan and built a cabin. Mr. Shaw quickly returned to Massachusetts and James stayed behind.

Anna's father's plan was for part of the family to establish the Michigan homestead while he and two of the sons stayed in Lawrence to work.

Twelve-year-old Anna, her two older sisters, younger brother, and mother left civilized Massachusetts and headed west. They knew little of farming, the dark forest, or the hard life that awaited them.

The pioneer life would have to be learned.
Like the right way to eat a banana.

They traveled by train as far as the rails would carry them into Michigan, where they were met by James. The group piled themselves and their possessions aboard a rough wagon and entered the woods. They were on their own—and would be for another year and a half.

"Fallen trees lay across our path, rivers caused long detours, while again and again we lost our way or were turned aside by impenetrable forest tangles," Anna recalled. "We sometimes had shelter, and sometimes failed to find it; sometimes we were fed, but often went hungry."

After many days, they reached their new home, a forlorn log cabin. Its windows and door were just cuts in the walls. Its floor was dirt. Water would have to be hauled from a distant stream. The cabin stood one hundred miles from the railroad, forty miles from a post office, and six miles from the nearest neighbor.

Anna's mother was shocked.

"I shall never forget the look my mother turned upon the place," Anna later remembered. "She crossed the threshold, and standing very still, looked slowly around her. Then something within her seemed to give way, and she sank upon the ground."

The children huddled quietly beside her as she lay in a heap. Night fell. Wildcats cried and wolves howled.

Finally, Anna's mother gathered herself together. "But her face never lost the deep lines those first hours of pioneer life cut upon it," said Anna.

The family set to work. Floorboards were laid in the house. Windows and a door were made. The cabin was divided into four rooms, and an attic was constructed.

Then James was injured and returned east. Anna, helped by her younger brother, Harry, took up the outdoor chores while her mother and older sisters tended the house.

Anna and Harry planted corn and potatoes by chopping the sod with an ax; the many tree stumps made plowing impossible.

They snared fish using wires removed from the girls' hoop skirts.

They collected sap from sugar maple trees in buckets, carried it home on yokes, and boiled it for sugar and syrup.

They gathered wild fruit.

They dug a well.

It was hard work, yet . . .

"Looking back upon those first months seems a long drawn-out and glorious picnic," Anna later said. "We had health, youth, enthusiasm, and good appetites."

What Anna didn't have was school.

But the family had books: histories, novels, and math texts.
"We read them until we knew them by heart," said Anna.
She also read the old newspapers that were hung in the cabin as wallpaper.

Despite the rigors of wilderness life, Anna discovered within herself the desire to "talk to people and tell them things."

"Just why, just what, I did not yet know, but I began to preach in the silent woods, to stand on stumps and address the unresponsive trees," Anna said.

When she was fifteen, Anna got her first chance to talk to people and tell them things. She became a teacher. Anna's simple education, self-made from her family's small library, earned her the job.

Anna became the mistress of a small log schoolhouse with fourteen students and a wood-burning stove. She provided her own books for the children's use and gathered logs for the stove. She earned two dollars a week.

Still, her ambition was not satisfied by her tiny audience of students. Anna
nearly lost heart and felt as rudderless as the crippled *John Jacob Westervelt* had
once been. She quit teaching and became a seamstress.

Then Anna met a woman minister, to whom she bared her dreams.
The minister replied, "My child, you can't do anything without an education.
Get it, and get it now!"

Encouraged by those wise words, Anna resumed the journey of her life and decided to enroll in college.

Graduating would be difficult, but Anna's confidence and optimism had been brightly polished by her pioneering years.

"The morning after my arrival on the campus, I saw a big copper penny lying on the ground, and, on picking it up, discovered that it bore the year of my birth," Anna said. "That seemed a good omen."

Eventually, she graduated from college and became a minister and, later, a doctor—careers that women were discouraged from entering at that time. Anna's pioneer experiences helped her brush aside the wrong-headed notions of those years. She understood that when there was work to be done, it didn't matter who swung the ax or pushed the shovel; the only demand was that the job get done.

It angered her that women worked "at half men's wages, not because their work was inferior, but because they were women," as Anna put it.

Anna vowed to open the minds of people who would hobble women's dreams. She believed that winning women the long-denied right to vote was the first step.

Anna carried the message everywhere. The little girl who had once preached to the hushed forest now spoke to audiences around the world. As with building a home in the wilderness, setbacks were frequent and successes came slowly and modestly. But Anna was untroubled. She was a pioneer.

Anna Howard Shaw battled for the vote until her death in 1919. That same year, the U.S. Congress voted in favor of the idea, and in 1920 a woman's right to vote became law.

By most measures, Anna Howard Shaw's life had been filled with struggle.

But Anna had used her own scale and had kept her own measurements, and that made all the difference—

to her and to us.

AUTHOR'S NOTE

Anna Howard Shaw was born in England in 1847.

By the time she was five, her family had emigrated to America and settled in Lawrence, Massachusetts. There the Shaws adopted the cause of abolition and hid runaway slaves in their house.

In 1859, Anna's father uprooted part of his family and resettled them in the wild Michigan woods. The heavy burden of carving out a homestead fell upon his wife, who had difficulty walking, and his younger children. Mr. Shaw and his family were reunited a year and a half later, but not for very long: he and his elder sons joined the Union Army during the Civil War and did not return for years.

Anna earned a theology degree from Boston University in 1878—the only woman in her class—and became a church minister. She later earned her medical degree but was never a practicing physician.

But Anna's life's work truly began when she embraced the cause of women's rights, especially the struggle to win the right to vote. She became a close colleague of leading suffragette Susan B. Anthony and replaced Anthony as president of the National American Woman Suffrage Movement at Anthony's death. Anna worked tirelessly for the cause for many years and gave thousands of lectures on its behalf.

Most of the material for *A Voice from the Wilderness: The Story of Anna Howard Shaw* was derived from Anna's autobiography, *The Story of a Pioneer*. Originally published in 1915, the book can be downloaded for free through the Project Gutenberg Web site at http://sailor.gutenberg.org.

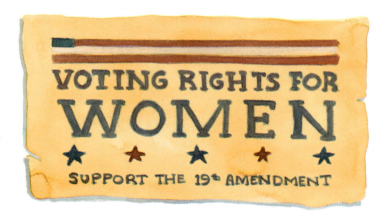